5 MINUTES BEFORE BED

Reflection and gratitude Journal for a happier you in just 5 minutes a Day

Date _____

Mood 😊 🙂 😐 🙁 😟

The best part of today was:

_____

_____

_____

Today's challenge(s) were:

5 small things I am grateful for today:

What did I take for granted today?

My favourite color today was:

Date _____

Mood

A mistake that I made today:

___

3 things that made me smile today:	The most fun thing today was:

Something beautiful that I saw today:	Modern invention I am grateful for today?

Date _____

Mood 😀 🙂 😐 🙁 ☹️

Favourite website today:

_____

Best things about my job today:

Top 5 songs today:

Favourite piece of clothing today?

Best gift someone could give me today?

Date _____

Mood   😞

The most special person today was:

_____
....
_____

2 people that was hard to get on today with:	One goal I can achieve before the end of the month?

Something I was good at today:	What smell am I grateful for today?

Date _____

Mood 😄 🙂 😐 🙁 ☹️

What made me most happy today was:

_____

_____

_____

If today I had $10,000 I would:	5 small things I need more of today:

One word that describes me today:

What I am looking forward to?

Date _____

Mood 🙂 🙂 😐 🙁 😟

The best part of today was:

_____

_____

Today's challenge(s) were:	5 small things I am grateful for today:

My favourite color today was:

What did I take for granted today?

Date _____

Mood

A mistake that I made today:

_____
_____
_____

3 things that made me smile today:	The most fun thing today was:

Something beautiful that I saw today:	Modern invention I am grateful for today?

Date _____

Mood 😃 🙂 😐 🙁 😟

Favourite website today:

Best things about my job today:

Top 5 songs today:

Favourite piece of clothing today?

Best gift someone could give me today?

Date _____

Mood

The most special person today was:

_____

_____

2 people that was hard to get on today with:	One goal I can achieve before the end of the month?

Something I was good at today:	What smell am I grateful for today?

Date _____

Mood 😊 🙂 😐 🙁 😟

What made me most happy today was:

_____

_____

If today I had $10,000 I would:

One word that describes me today:

---

5 small things I need more of today:

What I am looking forward to?

Date _____

Mood 😊 🙂 😐 🙁 ☹️

The best part of today was:

_____

_____

_____

Today's challenge(s) were:

5 small things I
am grateful for
today:

What did I take for
granted today?

My favourite color today was:

Date _____

Mood   🙁 🙁

A mistake that I made today:

_____

_____

3 things that made me smile today:	The most fun thing today was:

Something beautiful that I saw today:	Modern invention I am grateful for today?

Date _____

Mood 😀 😊 😐 🙁 ☹️

Favourite website today:

Best things about my job today:

Top 5 songs today:

Favourite piece of clothing today?

Best gift someone could give me today?

Date _____

Mood

The most special person today was:

_____

_____

2 people that was hard to get on today with:	One goal I can achieve before the end of the month?

Something I was good at today:	What smell am I grateful for today?

Date _____

Mood 😊 🙂 😐 🙁 ☹️

What made me most happy today was:

_____

_____

If today I had $10,000 I would:	5 small things I need more of today:

One word that describes me today:

What I am looking forward to?

Date _____

Mood 😊 🙂 😐 🙁 ☹️

The best part of today was:

_____

_____

_____

Today's challenge(s) were:

5 small things I am grateful for today:

My favourite color today was:

What did I take for granted today?

Date _____

Mood

A mistake that I made today:

---

3 things that made me smile today:	The most fun thing today was:

Something beautyful that I saw today:	Modern invention I am grateful for today?

Date _____

Mood 😃 😊 😐 🙁 ☹️

Favourite website today:

_____

_____

Best things about my job today:

Top 5 songs today:

Favourite piece of clothing today?

Best gift someone could give me today?

Date _____

Mood   😕 😖

The most special person today was:
_____
_____
_____

2 people that was hard to get on today with:	One goal I can achieve before the end of the month?

Something I was good at today:	What smell am I grateful for today?

Date _____

Mood 😊 🙂 😐 🙁 ☹️

What made me most happy today was:

_____

_____

_____

If today I had $10,000 I would:

5 small things I need more of today:

What I am looking forward to?

One word that describes me today:

Date _____

Mood 😊 🙂 😐 🙁 ☹️

The best part of today was:

_____

_____

Today's challenge(s) were:

5 small things I am grateful for today:

What did I take for granted today?

My favourite color today was:

Date _____

Mood

A mistake that I made today:

_____

_____

3 things that made me smile today:	The most fun thing today was:

Something beautiful that I saw today:	Modern invention I am grateful for today?

Date _____

Mood 😄 🙂 😐 🙁 ☹️

Favourite website today:

___

Best things about my job today:

Top 5 songs today:

Favourite piece of clothing today?

Best gift someone could give me today?

Date _____

Mood

The most special person today was:

_____

_____

2 people that was hard to get on today with:	One goal I can achieve before the end of the month?

Something I was good at today:	What smell am I grateful for today?

Date _____

Mood 😊 🙂 😐 🙁 ☹️

What made me most happy today was:

_____

_____

_____

If today I had $10,000 I would:	5 small things I need more of today:

One word that describes me today:

What I am looking forward to?

Date _____

Mood 😊 🙂 😐 🙁 ☹️

The best part of today was:

_____

_____

_____

Today's challenge(s) were:

5 small things I am grateful for today:

What did I take for granted today?

My favourite color today was:

Date _____

Mood   🙁 ☹

A mistake that I made today:

_____
_____
_____

3 things that made me smile today:	The most fun thing today was:

Something beautifyl that I saw today:	Modern invention I am grateful for today?

Date _____

Mood 😊 😊 😐 😕 ☹

Favourite website today:

_____

Best things about my job today:

Top 5 songs today:

Favourite piece of clothing today?

Best gift someone could give me today?

Date _____

Mood   😕 ☹

The most special person today was:

_____

_____

_____

2 people that was hard to get on today with:	One goal I can achieve before the end of the month?

Something I was good at today:	What smell am I grateful for today?

Date _____

Mood 🙂 😊 😐 🙁 ☹️

What made me most happy today was:

_____

_____

If today I had $10,000 I would:

5 small things I need more of today:

What I am looking forward to?

One word that describes me today:

Date _____

Mood 😃 😊 😐 🙁 😣

The best part of today was:

_____

_____

_____

Today's challenge(s) were:

5 small things I am grateful for today:

My favourite color today was:

What did I take for granted today?

Date _____

Mood

A mistake that I made today:

_____

_____

3 things that made me smile today:	The most fun thing today was:

Something beautiful that I saw today:	Modern invention I am grateful for today?

Date _____

Mood 😀 🙂 😐 🙁 ☹️

Favourite website today:

Best things about my job today:

Top 5 songs today:

Favourite piece of clothing today?

Best gift someone could give me today?

Date _____

Mood   🙁

The most special person today was:

_____

_____

_____

2 people that was hard to get on today with:	One goal I can achieve before the end of the month?

Something I was good at today:	What smell am I grateful for today?

Date _____

Mood 😀 🙂 😐 🙁 ☹️

What made me most happy today was:

_____

_____

_____

If today I had $10,000 I would:

5 small things I need more of today:

One word that describes me today:

What I am looking forward to?

Date _____

Mood 😊 🙂 😐 🙁 ☹️

The best part of today was:

_____

_____

Today's challenge(s) were:

5 small things I am grateful for today:

My favourite color today was:

What did I take for granted today?

Date _____

Mood

A mistake that I made today:

---

3 things that made me smile today:	The most fun thing today was:

Something beautifyl that I saw today:	Modern invention I am grateful for today?

Date _____

Mood 🙂 🙂 😐 🙁 ☹️

Favourite website today:

Best things about my job today:

Top 5 songs today:

Favourite piece of clothing today?

Best gift someone could give me today?

Date _____

Mood

The most special person today was:

_____

_____

2 people that was hard to get on today with:	One goal I can achieve before the end of the month?

Something I was good at today:	What smell am I grateful for today?

Date _____

Mood 😊 🙂 😐 🙁 ☹️

What made me most happy today was:

_____

_____

_____

If today I had $10,000 I would:

5 small things I need more of today:

What I am looking forward to?

One word that describes me today:

Date _____

Mood 😊 🙂 😐 🙁 😟

The best part of today was:

_____

_____

_____

Today's challenge(s) were:

5 small things I am grateful for today:

What did I take for granted today?

My favourite color today was:

Date _____

Mood

A mistake that I made today:

_____

_____

3 things that made me smile today:	The most fun thing today was:

Something beautiful that I saw today:	Modern invention I am grateful for today?

Date _____

Mood 😃 😊 😐 🙁 ☹️

Favourite website today:

Best things about my job today:

Top 5 songs today:

Favourite piece of clothing today?

Best gift someone could give me today?

Date _____

Mood

The most special person today was:

_____

_____

2 people that was hard to get on today with:	One goal I can achieve before the end of the month?

Something I was good at today:	What smell am I grateful for today?

Date _____

Mood 😃 🙂 😐 🙁 ☹️

What made me most happy today was:

_____

_____

_____

If today I had $10,000 I would:

5 small things I need more of today:

What I am looking forward to?

One word that describes me today:

Date _____

Mood 😊 🙂 😐 🙁 ☹️

The best part of today was:

_____

_____

_____

Today's challenge(s) were:

5 small things I am grateful for today:

What did I take for granted today?

My favourite color today was:

Date _____

Mood

A mistake that I made today:
_____
_____
_____

3 things that made me smile today:	The most fun thing today was:

Something beautiful that I saw today:	Modern invention I am grateful for today?

Date _____

Mood 😊 🙂 😐 🙁 ☹️

Favourite website today:

_____

_____

Best things about my job today:

Top 5 songs today:

Favourite piece of clothing today?

Best gift someone could give me today?

Date _____

Mood   😕 ☹

The most special person today was:

_____

_____

_____

2 people that was hard to get on today with:	One goal I can achieve before the end of the month?

Something I was good at today:	What smell am I grateful for today?

Date _____

Mood 😊 🙂 😐 🙁 ☹️

What made me most happy today was:

_____

_____

If today I had $10,000 I would:

5 small things I need more of today:

One word that describes me today:

What I am looking forward to?

Date _____

Mood 😃 🙂 😐 🙁 😟

The best part of today was:

....

....

....

Today's challenge(s) were:

5 small things I am grateful for today:

My favourite color today was:

What did I take for granted today?

Date _____

Mood

A mistake that I made today:

_____
_____

3 things that made me smile today:	The most fun thing today was:

Something beautifyl that I saw today:	Modern invention I am grateful for today?

Date _____

Mood 😀 🙂 😐 🙁 ☹️

Favourite website today:

_____

_____

_____

Best things about my job today:

Top 5 songs today:

Favourite piece of clothing today?

Best gift someone could give me today?

Date _____

Mood

The most special person today was:

_____
_____

2 people that was hard to get on today with:	One goal I can achieve before the end of the month?

Something I was good at today:	What smell am I grateful for today?

Date _____

Mood 😊 🙂 😐 🙁 ☹️

What made me most happy today was:

If today I had $10,000 I would:

5 small things I need more of today:

What I am looking forward to?

One word that describes me today:

Date _____

Mood 😃 😊 😐 🙁 😣

The best part of today was:

_____

_____

_____

Today's challenge(s) were:

5 small things I am grateful for today:

What did I take for granted today?

My favourite color today was:

Date _____

Mood

A mistake that I made today:

_____

_____

3 things that made me smile today:	The most fun thing today was:

Something beautiful that I saw today:	Modern invention I am grateful for today?

Date _____

Mood 😃 🙂 😐 🙁 ☹️

Favourite website today:

Best things about my job today:

Top 5 songs today:

Favourite piece of clothing today?

Best gift someone could give me today?

Date _____

Mood   :(:-(

The most special person today was:

_____

_____

2 people that was hard to get on today with:	One goal I can achieve before the end of the month?

Something I was good at today:	What smell am I grateful for today?

Date _____

Mood 😊 🙂 😐 🙁 ☹️

What made me most happy today was:

_____

_____

_____

If today I had $10,000 I would:

5 small things I need more of today:

What I am looking forward to?

One word that describes me today:

Date _____

Mood 😀 🙂 😐 🙁 ☹️

The best part of today was:

_____

_____

Today's challenge(s) were:

5 small things I am grateful for today:

What did I take for granted today?

My favourite color today was:

Date _____

Mood

A mistake that I made today:

_____

_____

3 things that made me smile today:	The most fun thing today was:

Something beautifyl that I saw today:	Modern invention I am grateful for today?

Date _____

Mood 😊 🙂 😐 🙁 ☹️

Favourite website today:

_____

_____

Best things about my job today:

Top 5 songs today:

Favourite piece of clothing today?

Best gift someone could give me today?

Date _____

Mood   😕 ☹

The most special person today was:

_____

_____

_____

2 people that was hard to get on today with:	One goal I can achieve before the end of the month?

Something I was good at today:	What smell am I grateful for today?

Date _____

Mood 😊 🙂 😐 🙁 ☹️

What made me most happy today was:

_____

_____

_____

If today I had $10,000 I would:	5 small things I need more of today:

One word that describes me today:

What I am looking forward to?

Date _____

Mood 😊 🙂 😐 🙁 ☹️

The best part of today was:

_____

_____

_____

Today's challenge(s) were:

5 small things I am grateful for today:

What did I take for granted today?

My favourite color today was:

Date _____

Mood

A mistake that I made today:

___

3 things that made me smile today:	The most fun thing today was:

Something beautiful that I saw today:	Modern invention I am grateful for today?

Date

Mood 😃 🙂 😐 🙁 ☹️

Favourite website today:

Best things about my job today:

Top 5 songs today:

Favourite piece of clothing today?

Best gift someone could give me today?

Date _____

Mood 😊 🙂 😐 🙁 ☹

The most special person today was:

_____

_____

2 people that was hard to get on today with:	One goal I can achieve before the end of the month?

Something I was good at today:	What smell am I grateful for today?

Date _____

Mood 😀 🙂 😐 🙁 ☹️

What made me most happy today was:

_____

_____

If today I had $10,000 I would:

5 small things I need more of today:

What I am looking forward to?

One word that describes me today:

Date _____

Mood 😊 🙂 😐 🙁 ☹️

The best part of today was:

_____

_____

_____

Today's challenge(s) were:	5 small things I am grateful for today:

My favourite color today was:

What did I take for granted today?

Date _____

Mood

A mistake that I made today:

_____

_____

3 things that made me smile today:	The most fun thing today was:

Something beautiful that I saw today:	Modern invention I am grateful for today?

Date _____

Mood 🙂 🙂 😐 🙁 ☹️

Favourite website today:

_____

Best things about my job today:	Top 5 songs today:

Best gift someone could give me today?

Favourite piece of clothing today?

Date _____

Mood

The most special person today was:

_____

_____

2 people that was hard to get on today with:	One goal I can achieve before the end of the month?

Something I was good at today:	What smell am I grateful for today?

Date _____

Mood 🙂 🙂 😐 🙁 ☹️

What made me most happy today was:

_____

_____

If today I had $10,000 I would:	5 small things I need more of today:

One word that describes me today:

What I am looking forward to?

Date _____

Mood 😃 🙂 😐 🙁 ☹️

The best part of today was:

_____

_____

Today's challenge(s) were:	5 small things I am grateful for today:

My favourite color today was:

What did I take for granted today?

Date _____

Mood

A mistake that I made today:

_____

_____

_____

3 things that made me smile today:	The most fun thing today was:

Something beautiful that I saw today:	Modern invention I am grateful for today?

Date _____

Mood 😃 😊 😐 🙁 😣

Favourite website today:

_____

_____

_____

Best things about my job today:

Top 5 songs today:

Favourite piece of clothing today?

Best gift someone could give me today?

Date _____

Mood   😕 😣

The most special person today was:

_____

_____

_____

2 people that was hard to get on today with:	One goal I can achieve before the end of the month?

Something I was good at today:	What smell am I grateful for today?

Date _____

Mood 😃 🙂 😐 🙁 😟

What made me most happy today was:

_____
....
_____

If today I had $10,000 I would:

5 small things I need more of today:

One word that describes me today:

What I am looking forward to?

Date _____

Mood 😀 🙂 😐 🙁 ☹️

The best part of today was:

_____

_____

Today's challenge(s) were:	5 small things I am grateful for today:

My favourite color today was:

What did I take for granted today?

Date _____

Mood

A mistake that I made today:

_____
_____

3 things that made me smile today:	The most fun thing today was:

Something beautiful that I saw today:	Modern invention I am grateful for today?

Date _____

Mood 😊 🙂 😐 🙁 ☹️

Favourite website today:

_____

_____

_____

Best things about my job today:

Top 5 songs today:

Favourite piece of clothing today?

Best gift someone could give me today?

Date _____

Mood

The most special person today was:

_____

_____

_____

2 people that was hard to get on today with:	One goal I can achieve before the end of the month?

Something I was good at today:	What smell am I grateful for today?

Date _____

Mood 😊 🙂 😐 🙁 ☹️

What made me most happy today was:

_____

_____

If today I had $10,000 I would:	5 small things I need more of today:

One word that describes me today:

What I am looking forward to?

Date _____

Mood 😃 🙂 😐 🙁 😣

The best part of today was:

Today's challenge(s) were:

5 small things I am grateful for today:

What did I take for granted today?

My favourite color today was:

Date _____

Mood   🙁 ☹️

A mistake that I made today:

___

3 things that made me smile today:	The most fun thing today was:

Something beautiful that I saw today:	Modern invention I am grateful for today?

Date _____

Mood 😊 🙂 😐 🙁 ☹️

Favourite website today:

_____

_____

_____

Best things about my job today:

Top 5 songs today:

Favourite piece of clothing today?

Best gift someone could give me today?

Date _____

Mood

The most special person today was:

_____

_____

2 people that was hard to get on today with:	One goal I can achieve before the end of the month?

Something I was good at today:	What smell am I grateful for today?

Date _____

Mood 😀 🙂 😐 🙁 😦

What made me most happy today was:

If today I had $10,000 I would:

5 small things I need more of today:

What I am looking forward to?

One word that describes me today:

Date _____

Mood 😊 🙂 😐 🙁 😟

The best part of today was:

_____

_____

Today's challenge(s) were:

5 small things I am grateful for today:

What did I take for granted today?

My favourite color today was:

Date _____

Mood

A mistake that I made today:

___

3 things that made me smile today:	The most fun thing today was:

Something beautiful that I saw today:	Modern invention I am grateful for today?

Date _____

Mood 😊 🙂 😐 🙁 ☹️

Favourite website today:

_____

_____

Best things about my job today:	Top 5 songs today:

Favourite piece of clothing today?

Best gift someone could give me today?

Date _____

Mood   😕 ☹

The most special person today was:

_____

_____

2 people that was hard to get on today with:	One goal I can achieve before the end of the month?

Something I was good at today:	What smell am I grateful for today?

Date _____

Mood 🙂 🙂 😐 🙁 ☹️

What made me most happy today was:

_____

_____

_____

If today I had $10,000 I would:

5 small things I need more of today:

What I am looking forward to?

One word that describes me today:

Date _____

Mood 😀 😊 😐 🙁 ☹️

The best part of today was:

_____

_____

Today's challenge(s) were:

5 small things I am grateful for today:

What did I take for granted today?

My favourite color today was:

Date _____

Mood

A mistake that I made today:

_____
_____
_____

3 things that made me smile today:	The most fun thing today was:

Something beautiful that I saw today:	Modern invention I am grateful for today?

Date _____

Mood 😀 🙂 😐 🙁 ☹️

Favourite website today:

Best things about my job today:

Top 5 songs today:

Favourite piece of clothing today?

Best gift someone could give me today?

Date _____

Mood

The most special person today was:

_____

_____

_____

2 people that was hard to get on today with:	One goal I can achieve before the end of the month?

Something I was good at today:	What smell am I grateful for today?

Printed in Poland
by Amazon Fulfillment
Poland Sp. z o.o., Wrocław